Late News From Britain

C. J. P. Smith

ACKNOWLEDGEMENTS are due to the following publications in which some of these poems have appeared: *Acumen* and *The Interpreter's House.*

'Mam Tor', 'Cymru Nouveaux', 'Not Circe' and 'The Slow Worm' appeared in *Mushroom Lane,* Acumen poetry pamhlet 1.

British Library C-i-P data:
A catalogue record for this book is
available from the British Library.

ISBN: 978 - 1 - 873161 - 41 - 8

Published by
ACUMEN PUBLICATIONS, 6 The Mount, Higher Furzeham,
Brixham, South Devon TQ5 8QY, UK.

CONTENTS:

Places, people

Wildlife

Poems from the South West

PLACES, PEOPLE

Late News from Britain

In Britain, now what have we to fear?
Our leaders only give their ear
to great King Arthur, or good King Lear.

Under plate glass and steel, stale Victoriana,
lurching over cobbles in Mermaid Yard,
kneeling alone in a cracked gothic church,
stirring red waters in the Roman bath.
I popped a cork for Cymbeline between those breasted hills
and at the sea's edge heard sunken bells.

We can barely shift for ruin –
trampled stone, mud, the map's impositions,
straightjacket elm darkening field boundaries,
permafrost of re-used streets, preservations.
This island bites its own tail, breathes changelessly.
Twenty centuries dining out on the world –
bringing the invader's voice to fit these contours,
the spun globe always-already at the door,
another bloodbath on the Saxon Shore?

Yet in Britain what have we to fear?
What aspect should our culture wear
when warriors take their beef and beer
with old King Arthur and good King Lear?

The Archaeologist

I pressed my ear to the broken earth
and heard all the blood rusted locks
of ancient Rome
turn once.

I spread this bead of charcoal across my palm,
and smelled the tang
of fallen beams
in Camulodunum.

The name rolled over and over, charred in fame,
like a gnarled root in a riverbed.

Then I sketched the *via principia*,
the post holes, the ditches, washed the dirt
from blue glass beads, *mortaria*

and asked once, why I did this,
could only answer with a shrug
and threw some comment about what we think we know,
picking out a brooch clasp from the spoil.

Since then, the profiles of emperors
stare impassively, upwards in cold air
at high, indifferent, clouds
as if something, just out of field, had collectively slipped
their minds.

Brittunculi

The Eagles sailed into our thoughts –
whoever we once were –
and somehow our ancestors,
our blood, our language,
bought into the newly-branded peace.

And at the till of time
some barcode print of DNA
shows up the staining of a culture never pure,
languages' promiscuities and roots,
the shiftings and blendings,
contexts which flash evanescent
into the leafy edges of the great woodlands.
Hoofbeats in the dusk.
Little Britons on the margins of becoming.

Roman Fort, Castleton

Down there,
two hidden streams, a river valley,
elder bushes bent double
with glassy beads of wine.

From this grassy platform
you can see every hilltop.
The rings of the Tor –
hammered bronze –
are elegant in their pursuit of the curve
alongside this blank regularity.

If we could put back the walls –
three hundred odd years
of comings and goings –
four-square supervision of every breath –
slaves, cattle, digging lead –
and that noisy wattle village
sprawling round the perimeter,
how would it look then
to Sunday walkers feeding sensibilities
on fragments and follies?

Frost

The dead huddle together behind broken palings
wearing only angels and obelisks
stained in someone else's time.
Hanging around on eternal parole,
giving out clipped biographies
defaced by birth and death and love.
The shortest marks of what they were.

Some have slipped from the crowd,
rejected this wealthy colonial pastiche,
this chainstore Gothic.
They lounge against a rough wall
braiding roots torn from holly and hawthorn,
peering from the dry brown froth of sapless bindweed.

All night and all morning
they have rolled themselves up in ice
leaving humps and hollows on the grass
for the light to fetch.
One, over there, is raising an ash tree
to keep away the sun.

They are trying, disgracefully, to get straight
all that was said in their gutted church,
and what it meant for them alone,
but prefer instead
to seep into the polished matrix
and split the letter from the stone.

Sometimes they look up at the blackened spire
and the sun's disc
rusting day and night together.
But memories are shapeless, corroded,
you can never pick them from the ground
where your eyes dig.

Poet on the Street

That tiny, two-storey house
derelict, on Carver Street, has gone.
Its skull windows and scrawny elder bush
now make room for grinding tyres,
glass, chippings kicked between cobbles;
old street lines too ingrained to shift.
The car park is an oblong
with no reminders, no problem plots.

Outside the library, hawking his own verse
is a man four weeks fresh from Ireland.
Poetry he sells for food; tiny pamphlets.
Said he'd shifted maybe even a thousand –
for each one taken, a straight English pound.

He says *all poets are cans of worms*
other poets can't really bear:
and to most other folks it looks
as if they all think life's a stroll in the park.

But then people want a laugh between chores
or good words done for them cheap
with no shrapnel – *someone else to take it on the chin,
and you know son, the thing is, that's where we come in.*

Springvale Road to Burngreave

The sky has cleared.
I'm glad for that; and the moon,
lolling back drunk in its armchair
watches the stars outshine this city height
and the outlines of terraces and church towers
cut crisply from the night.

Down Attercliffe, and the Don,
the whole city-bed shimmers
like a brazier, scattered, kicked over.

Burngreave Cemetery

Here by the boarded-up church
I struck an old memory with the tip of my boot –
a child's gaze waiting inside a car
while grandmother paid her dues
escorted from the banked path to stoop down
reverentially, with sweet flowers we abuse
for birth and marriage, death and love.

She wore that real fur coat
and dangling stole,
some tawny chic relic,
she had preserved away
which filled me with a small boy's horrors
(complete with fox's head and paws).

Wrapped up like Tamora, Queen of the Goths,
making a progress to her father's cross,
with hatpins, gloves, scarf and scent
and moths.

Nocturne – The Lodge, 1972

Summer log fires initiated those acolytes –
youthful shadows leaping from the walls,
failing in every slender crack of split twig.

Blackened pans gurgled, sparked and sputtered.

Baroque arpeggios brought down snowflakes
hard around those skeletal towers of elm
and logsmoke swept low through bramble ribs.

They were, they said, artists, visionaries and dreamers,
half-deified by candle tongues and mirrors,
draining the last bottle of those squandered hours.

Two hundred years behind the times – the future lours,
under star-frosted skies and green apple showers.

The Invigilator

1.
Two kinds of time inhabit these rooms:
mine is the great slow stream;
yours, counts the minutes with a biro point
and a hard focus, burning up the paper.
Run fingers across your scalp
looking for the roots of answers.
Put your hands on your head
thoughts will flap away like butterflies.
Rub your mouth with the back of your hand –
you are not dreaming. Avoid my gaze.
Crack your knuckles, break open questions.
Roll your eyes to the ceiling like an El Greco Christ,
sigh from magma depths and pluck at your lips,
suck your pen for the nipple of a mother's help,
the child who should have worked but only larked.

2.
Musicians fill the hot upper room in the 1890s house
teasing out ghostly tinklings of notes through headphones,
new mysteries from *Korg* and *Yamaha,*
under those delicate flourishes of hands
create invisible electrical beings,
striving to 'Complete this bourrée in the manner of Bach'.

For Edward Thomas

I can't help liking Edward Thomas:
remembering those moody boots
tramping across his overgrown island
among nettles, farmsteads and wild hedges
patient in dereliction and neglect,
digging people's words back into history
twisting together the pen and the plough,
listening with respect
to languages other than ours
betrayed to him only in bright calls
of birds, and leaves, and unknown powers.

I just can't help it – liking Edward Thomas –
for the way he tried and failed to be Welsh:
complicating, as he went, notions of Englishness
for academics
and refusing to murder cats that ate nightingales –
oh, and his love of Wales.

Oh yes, I do like Edward Thomas –
he's a very good poet to sulk with –
especially during rain, as is Verlaine.

The Ultra-Moderns have no time for Thomas,
still finding him very *fin de siècle*
and of course they heckle.
but looking further they discover
like everyone else, he took his chance
with *différance*.

Yes, I do remember:
even Leavis scrutinised Edward Thomas, sure,
half-ordained him into the Great Gang of literature,
and was fairly happy to let him pass
into the dead, yet priestly, cast.

But I'll read Edward Thomas,
nevertheless.

The First World War in Colour

Somebody might still just have known them,
soldier or civilian,
blown petals from the pink cherry –
October leaves lying along a stream bed,
faces flittering like bats' wings
trapped between those few seconds of antique light
and the burnt gradations locked immobile into ciné reels.
How they may come back at our behest
to work the dire comedies of the past.

Look how the fields swell with grey uniforms,
how the great red grape of the nineteenth century
burst its lewd fashions into our memory,
Twentieth, Twenty-first,
us and our desperate thirst for keeping history.

Europeans posturing in ostrich feathers,
Archdukes, Kaisers,
great uncle Tommy Atkins standing up alive
pulling on a muddy fag, camouflaged forever.
How his mates march and totter, shoot and shatter,
parade and stagger, blast, rot.

Some always grin at the camera,
some are beyond fatigue.
Their nations, like good nurses,
topped them up to the tonsils with the old lies.
We watch them from our other rooms long distance,
as they come on again,
like eager passengers to the shore of the last black river.

Searching for the Tennyson Room, Usher Gallery, Lincoln

Once, the ephemera of Laureateship,
dryly fluttering its wings behind glass cases,
conveyed a fading but palpable sense of awe –
a delicate rich smell of age and polish.

Pipes and pens, monographs and illustrations,
familial photographs, the state funeral in the cold Abbey
everything as black as coal soot from a grate –
the Great Man's hat and Spanish cloak –
its lining like a Tiger Moth's underwing –
Grand Patriarch posing as gypsy,
dark Nosferatu of elegiac metre
conjuring rhythmical echoes –
dactylic clatter of carriage wheels carrying Maud.

Years have collapsed to nothings,
creak of oak, cool harmony:
clock time in the Usher Gallery.

Half a league onwards into a new age
they have recast that little room,
made it over into the compulsory fun of coloured space,
some telescreen braying interactively to itself
while Tennyson sulks in the knocked-up lock up
where *no splendour falls.*

Shoved behind the scruffy art room space,
with the smells of stale cigarettes,
Victoria's Laureate of Darkness –
a cape on a headless dummy, put aside,
stopping a hole to keep the past away.

Byron's Old Place, Newstead Abbey

All the family gods transfix the air
and somewhere beyond their painted stares
we only read his love and his despair,
the deadly playful gaze of the tiger.

His one secure belief,
like violent passion in the blood:
immortal poetry – human frailty,
human falsehood.

Peasant Poet

Leave poor old Clare alone, he's withered to the bone,
lost his way like a wagtail, trotting home.
We can't heal John Clare, and you don't really care,
just try to comprehend – his grief will never end.

Leave poor old Clare alone, his world turned bleak as bone,
this tender labourer's son thought he was Lord Byron.
His head stayed full of love and fields and birds,
the tears in his pockets spilled out words –
the world had to lock him up of course,
contain the infamy of God's curse,
and that dire longing for the voice
of his beloved Mary Joyce.

A Little Piece of Skiddaw

This mountain is hard asleep
not even bothering to laugh
at human history with a sheep's cough
in a cackle of scree
or to blow fresh clouds around the shattered pine rods.

Water takes flight,

sparkling and shivering

haring down over old fissures

to swill across my boots
and take any splashings I can make
with my fists full of broken rock.

The summit is indifferent to the stories of gods.

The whole monster, on its knees and elbows
sprawls with a kind of indolence I admire:

crouches under heather and stone –
would take my breath or break my bone
if I stole a piece and took it home.

Night Pilot, Shaldon

The world is black, cold, sunken,
menaced by cliffs of red sand.

All philosophy sits in the shadows
or slops over the dredged stage.

Rings of light ripple on the water
moving like watersnakes in the deep channel

coiled old ideas repeating new truths,
proven, resolved, legitimate –

forerunners of that elephantine bulk
looming in from the salty dark.

Mam Tor

Some minor Gog idly drew the earth rings on this hilltop
poked the stub-ends of its fingers hard into the chilled turf
so that from the air the pilot's lens says this was a settlement
a village perched up over the oval valley
watching sheep and cattle or strangers.

Going up lifts the air from your body.
Sitting still freezes the bones.
But then there was shelter perhaps
from the racing air which has bent these grasses
or the flying snow of hikers' chatter inside the ramparts
whose worn human burr of huts and walls
talks back only in patterns, obdurate recoveries.

Roadside Shrine

That yellow patch of clipped grass
lies decorated with a careful litter
of wilting flower heads in rain-soaked bunches.

They have slept out all night
with little messages of love
beside the ravening tyres.

Cymru Nouveaux

I'm sick of hearing the New Celts –
up from Oxford or the Goddoddin,
with their talk of torques
and poets who are really politicians.
Their chariots are hung with bronzes
(Welsh classes on a Tuesday night),
their voices like geese, and their armour
painted with whinges.

Listen, we are off to the wars,
with pothouse democrats,
heroes with biceps as broad
as their salaries in legend.
Look at the sea of drooping moustaches,
gifts of Caradoc, Llewellyn, Ap Rhys,
they lie dead as the pits
sucked out by the English.

It is the men of Cattraeth
who hate Swansea Jacks:
and the woebegone scribes of Bangor
who hate everyone.
The isle of Mona is sunk like a cowpat
under the weight of the Roman dead
and the hosts of women,
oaks, mistletoe, cars, ice cream.

Morgannwg runs her department
with Fair Trade coffee, theory and racial awareness,
she being from Camden
of quaint Welsh blood, a noble house.
At night she unzips the sea
and lets out the warriors
who it is said, have learnt the past tense only,
to pick coal and broken needles from the sand.

Two red kites are flying over Crai.
London lads really,
twisting their bodies
as the beaks shear down
and the landscape rolls its hips.

And yet, I love the green rivers and water-voices
free of old taints, industry and druids.
You can, it is said, sometimes fish there in absolute peace.

Not Circe

You are my secret love.
In the middle of the day,
sleeping, waking, there always
a face that does not steal away.

I have tried. I have fought you
with indifference, like death,
with I dare not, like choice,
with I cannot, like reason,
with dumbness, like love.

I kept you in a hazel-shell,
having shaken out the rain,
but it was so very heavy,
it breaks inside like dull barbs.

When you ran off
I found a scallop
and pushed you out,
but the water turned to lead.

Looking down from the plane
I saw your name
waiting, in the voices of the mountains,

the cobalt sea, the oriole.

Then you turned from a corn-sheaf
to a cat on my window.
It came inside and wouldn't budge,
even when I threw a dream at it.

Then you said "no more."
"No more." But the rainstorm wept.
The trees you bent double
only stroked my neck.
The sea stayed in the moon

where you left it.
"Yes" you said. "Yes."

In my head you planted a kiss.
You forgot this. It burned like phosphor,
made me dumb like an earthworm
tricked up by a bird's foot.
Now see. You, with your forgotten kiss.
You are careless and think me blind.
My ash has settled in your hair
and tonight I will have you back.

Overheard in Company of the Gentlemen Duellists of Duke Humphrey's Library, Oxford.

Prized and revered, privileges of silence:
all-comers remain interlopers and strangers:
closed books stand like musty butlers
witnessing shifts of readership;
trends, fashions, career trajectories.

And already, my neighbour is asleep,
leather tomes rise around him on sponge supports
as he lists to starboard, taking in air,
drowsing on summer pollen;
his gentle snores flit in and out like swallows.

This letter was *carried by Coleridge.*
Some of the ragged edges and bindings
crumble into my lap as I read...

"Since you arrived here," said an angry voice,
lunging fiercely out behind the shelves,
"you have behaved with an impeccable arrogance,
and somebody should make you dance!"

The owner, a bearded latterday Tradescant,
called to account the tall striped Curmudgeon,
the colleague with the drinker's complexion
and the studied *hauteur* of the bad librarian.

The boozer showed his hand at once:
"I'm late, so what, big deal, you ponce."
"I'll bust your head, I'll bust your face,
I'm sick of you and this damn place!"

Then out came Blackbeard's swashing blow,
a riposte like a javelin throw.
"Do you feel put on, victimised, abused?
"I am the one who is being used!

"If you want a fight, let's have it so,
"but it won't be *fisticuffs* you know."

So one grey morning in damp Port Meadow
perhaps they stood there, fellow to fellow,
with a box of flintlocks, or a pair of foils
and put an end to Oxford broils.

Gawping off Mam Tor

A vixen and cubs scarper
as my boots thud against stones and ruts
on the raised slopes.
All the valley mist is knapped
into fields ringed by stone and wire
and sheep in the distance bulge
like a bee-swarm pouring from their enclosure
under shouts and fists of herders
whose vague and distant echoes
drag down years, reusing the air itself,
making the earth underfoot chime
a temporary challenge to the sculpting wind.

WILDLIFE

Froglet

As you grow, this grass Amazon
bleaches around you.

Now your size outbids spiders
but yields to snake-forks and bird-beaks.

You stare, hearing brass in human voices,
at fingers searching the iron seed heads.

You are a spilt miracle of bronze,
a molten dribble of fresh metal juice,
fluid, splay-footed, your wide snout and all
tumbling mercurially into the quench of dew-beads.

Buzzard and Moon

Because of dusk under the jab of my pen
lost millennia flood the creased black hills
right to the foot of my creamy garden plot.

Pin-prick windows twinkle
down where pheasants vanish into briar clumps
and years tumble among the thighs of oaks,
all landscape couched as one splayed body
running to half light under giant cloud.

The moon spins its pocked-marked lure,
its muse's glamour painted over luteous bone,
drawing out some great reluctant bird from damps and leaf,
pushing off from the ledge of my own eye.

Grasshopper Warbler

Out there, dark, silence, dust and cold –
the universe huddled yellow around this halo;
summer light behind an elder bush
creamy with blossom.

Ventriloquising the sun's voice.
Planetary stutterings.
Undeviating morse.

Bullfinches

I cast about,
my eyes dowsing for the source
of that low whistle
now in the haw bushes, green thorns,
the tough bramble tops.
But nothing shows until bullfinches
settle round the dandelions.

She watches reverentially, patient as a stone –
he cranes his neck around, suspicious,
sidles up the stalks, tips the seed clocks into range
of delicate bill-nibblings
which mutually beard their beaks with fluff –
till what is merely sharing food
begins to look a bit like love?

Blackbird Singing

Blackbird shapes the song of rain.
Keeps the sounds of drizzling garden taps
for a warm evening in late spring.
Makes elegies from rain that will arrive –
and his dark blues is told worldwide.

Greenfinches

That long inevitable summer,
wandering lanes by the still canal
pursuers of wings flitting into hawthorn.

Skirting these semi-dormant farms,
and arid fields mourning calloused hands,
past a lock-house out of time.

Change slows to the palette of local places
and greenfinches up in the poplars
rehearse their nasal syllables
equivalent to the moment.

Two hundred odd years laid out:
sweet as the dead.

Pygmy Shrew

Miniature agitation of breath,
navigating gigantic swards of stalks
prying into every snuffed hollow
with a nose half a body-length again

delicate and prehensile, curving back to sniff.

A dropped sloe brings all this up short.

Provokes a dive
into bunched
roots.

Your tiny nerve-driven patter
hampered by rainforests of grass stalks

shivers at every sound
backs away,
chiding your own fanged mask in a water bead.

Starlings

Starlings waggle their beards
in the black willow,
whistling the afternoon over
tracing out their constellated name,
marked on the path below
in little white spats.

One Morning

Somewhere above the roar of city urgencies
a robin is dreaming
over its own jazz ragas
and cloud masses that Poussin set out
with Stoic formality
crash and glare with brilliant light
tearing all design apart;

silent, endless, inhuman art.

Peacetime

In that sudden brief moment of sun
a thrush flew up
onto the fence rail
chasing the million little flies
drifting about like seeds
around the sycamore clusters.

The young summer cloaks
victim and hunter alike-
the sparrowhawk working its theatre of leaf.
That green stalk snapped off by the wind
hangs shrivelled and desiccate,
even on this beautiful morning
when a chaffinch repeats the only poem it knows
and the thrushes ancient mysteries,
given freely out, slip away unread
by a nation with its eyes on ledgers and lies.

Sun is playing games
with light that slants or glares,
until I half believe that this green silence
always was complete
and the silhouetted warbler
eagerly feeding in the boughs
is somehow the mark of things that may keep
beyond this drifting peacetime
for at least as long as these insect clouds
pass and re-pass
the laurel, the holly and the ash
on the outside of the glass.

Redbreast

Every night, under the streetlamps,
a redbreast has been whistling in the snow
on a dead elm bough that catches the yellow glow –
singing neither for pay nor wages of any sort –
nothing that can be sold or bought,
till city, stone and branches break –
whatever noises humans make.

Not Saying Good Morning to the Magpies

Watch them.

See how they crop up in treetops:

how they bounce and drop,

taking down the daylight in a haggard rime of roadkill.

Watch them:

because it seems plain
how they understand
crow wings of burst tyres by the carriageway,
rusted litter of past moments,
the fox cub drowsing, still, cold, perfect.

The blank honest idiolect of death and life.

The Slow Worm

This quiet cleft in the hills
echoes to voices and a mongrel's bark
and my boot-trails swishing through fern
catching off rills and droplets
that the weak sun leaves to lie stark
like this poor worm,
a battered wand of bronze
I plucked from the cwm-side track
and set upon a withered bracken fan
as a moment's novelty
a suggestion only, life trodden from it,
of bright activity, wisdom, sagacity,
beyond our random ways.

I cradle its death in my love and wonder
that can only stroke and press this verse,
but make no quickening turn.

A golden eagle

skimming the stiff wind coming keen up the valley
twisting its thick neck, scrying the heather.

Big as a man in plumage,
hanging in feathered heaviness
nailed up stock still to the bulge
of the mountain's foot
while its vile eyes played about,
so that roads and cars were nothing
beside that long sweep that took it
down, fast, away, towards the water.

When it returned,
it held a slumped corpse
gripped in a crate of talons,
performing for the bread and circuses crowd
in a grim Coliseum of fells.

POEMS from the SOUTH WEST

Over the Border at Holcombe Rogus

In these blue hills and waters I met up with the old silences,
the indices of deep and ancient lanes,
this fell blue light and hidden river runnings,
cattle wild in the coombes,
skulls and bones up at the church, placed on graves,
The Holcombe Giant straddling the lanes,
Monk's wood, badger's dusk, black cat dark,
green crickets bringing old hedge lines alive
with rasping consonants, monosyllabic raffia soliloquies,
the song of leaf silhouettes in Rackham shadow.

Twilight at Holcombe Rogus

Let us take the oath then brothers,
whilst hedge crickets chirp their papery syllables into this
electric dusk.
Let us drink until we brawl and quibble or wrangle over
some point of art,
set right some detail of style from a lost and broken culture
placed before us in a book.

God is not dead, merely shouting in the dark.
Tomorrow we will sit all the day sipping lemon water to
cool our bellies,
a good life, not to weaken or relent
and when friends arrive, a walk, and a late, late dinner,
beyond exhaustion.

Here there is nothing to serve but laughter.

Appley

The lane to Appley walks you back two thousand years.
It's like an old airy barn that no-one uses,
trickling rain water and mud along
as the walls rise up and stand solid,
and yet today it runs as dry and hard as set lime.
People made it back then,
surely as people use it now,
not to walk it, but to race cars over red mud,
not to stop and touch the clustered hawthorns,
the little spring oak, ash saplings, cowslips,
the mesh of centuries expressed in green leaf;
a duck's nest; crickets, ticking the clock hands
of one more afternoon of freedom.

Eyes adjust to the cool dark.
All purpose drains from what was thought;
what you came here for, why you paused,
all irrelevant, as the cider tap springs its drowse
into cool miraculous golden columns of glass.

A Winter's Day,

We opened this late afternoon Book of Hours
upon ice and frost and brown deer
grazing the slopes
on the far side of the moor,
slanting their necks
as the slanting snow flew,
a partial glimpse of some antique world.

We fooled around;
jumping down hard upon the trackways
until the ice in the rhynes creaked
and the ground itself buoyed up.
We picked boulders the size of human heads
and hurled them into the ice
where they stuck, fixed like Dante's damned.

Cold, mist, snow flecks, hard earth
ice in the deep ditches trapping boulders,
puddles frozen into plate armour,
we lifted them whole, smashed them, ice upon ice,
delight and laughter in that abandoned place

all fell to silence in this great half-tamed swamp
a giant artless sump of mud life
decorated with swan necks and duck flocks
and willow shapes disfigured into beauty
by the hefted blade,
forming up places for black water to run back
when the bursted rivers reopen their banks
and life floods in again with the flanks of cattle.

The Cider Sheds, Curload

Those hands had bundled withies since childhood,
had taken the hooked blade to the sap,
had woven the funnelled elver-traps
set down in the rivers and rhynes
God's bounty for the Saxons,
sons of the yellow straw and the green hay.
Every year he gathered in what was here.

These patched sheds he inherited from old;
these casks his grandfather made,
and now, see how the oak is turning to earth,
see how the golden cider blackens overnight;
one short glassful,
brewed on its own orchard sugars,
wasp weary, windfall heavy,
holding the landscape in its ferment,
waiting to be clear and gold as the sunball.

His hands dusted off the hen nest,
the hay-clumps and spider kingdoms,
rinsed out one dubious glass
and proffered cider from an oak tap.

Its language was sharp, astringent,
it told of other stories, other times,
it reached always backwards,
always eloquently dumb.

Two Nocturnes:

West Sedgemoor

Moonlight spills across
bootmarks on the sodden grass,
over reed blades worked by the silversmith
and the voices of snipe, curlew,
describe the human form, what it might be,
set in a different confluence of being,
raised up alive from shadows alone.

Wandering out in defiance of the clock
over ruts and swards and lanes,
filled to the eyes like the rhynes
with mist or bird calls,
or some other darker language
which has no names like these.

The Wood-Yard, West Sedgemoor

Tonight, the moon is like –
the mask of a fox –
caught in its own light,
bounding from a clump of docks.

Tonight your long promised fire
exposes the old gods, loitering in hawthorn and ash:
black cats with eyes like molten wire
come bursting from that otherworld,
scattering plovers in their field of mire.

Tonight, lying on the warm earth, I broke bread
and looked into the flames
glittering and leaping in my glass again
and tried to reconcile
a silvery field of drenched cowslips
with the perpetual hiss of engines,
and distant orange lamps camped due west,
like some ancient army
putting back the sunrise with laughter
and boasts.

Pilgrimage to Watchet

Saint Decuman came ashore on a raft with a cow,
crossed the blue channel on a drift of logs.

He fled Wales and his all too worldly companions,
their lusts for gold, honeyed wine and the crying music of
the flesh.

His family mourned their lost Decumanus,
and here on the pagan shore he lived as a holy man,

a hermit, pouring out the blood of the White Christ,
from his battered Roman Samian.

Some local chap, a fine fellow, good with a blade,
a certain man more venomous than an asp,
more poisonous than the adder,
cut through his neck as he prayed.

Decuman bore off his head and bathed it in the holy well,
and from that moment flourished like the Green man,
and the work of God rose up from the sand
from the blown chaff of vulgar sin and guilt.

But this is not the sea-swallowed church he built.

Now we listen to our own parables, our own poet saints,
the old beautiful lies of the Mariner,

wind in the marram grass, the poet's song –
here things do not keep, or they keep too long.

Kilve to Nether Stowey

This soft powdery blue stone is bluer when wet
and outshone by the summer sky.
The sea shatters, fizzes and clears over rock pools
and gullies, scouring off blue mud;
salt water pale blue as liquid glass.
In the lane hawthorns hang bread-scented florets
down into faces lined by salt breezes.
Everything flowers out. The earth is trying to sing.
Summer winds search out the past through carved ivy
but cars barge in everywhere.
Medieval whispers rise beyond earshot over ruined gables
and the Chantry farm boasts one giant dangerous pig.
At Stowey, the 'dear gutters' run on from Coleridge's place.
Fragments cling to the hot daylight.
A sword he once held. Unread pages. Smallpox deaths.
Visions blow around like laundry while the locals serve up
                                    fake cream teas,
and the bookless shoulder of Somerset drowses, arid, eventless.
The land still waits to be worked.
For the touch of the deep plough.
For some deep touch of the inked plough.

Nightingale Country

In a paused heartbeat
nightingales' voices break cover.

Their calls erupt like flowers on green umbellifers,
in the time of bluebells' embellishments
of woodland floors; their cadences
creep into the capillaries of leaf,
along arteries of twig and thorn;
where those songs halt or waver, the afternoon palls.

Then later, under the liquid moon,
these woods are a library of song, the same birds
pricking out the velvet silence with excavated stars.

Time Paused at Blue Anchor

In a backyard of pub tables and drained pints,
sun already westering on a hot afternoon,
beating up fishy stinks from nets and bins,
threadbare conversations are picked over
and half-energised by known jokes,
laughter let out on a rickety old jaunt.

Four o'clock relaxes its elbows on warm sticky wood,
drinks go down a treat in this nowhere back street,
of empty crab claws and shrub flowers
all full of sunshine and lost destinations,
lost aspirations.

The Cider God

The breeze that stirs the withies on the moor
catches up a heron, stiffly oaring its bulk into the air.
Cloud castles build into sunburst afternoons
and moorhens nod across rhyne sedges.
Work lies close to the thick mud
and in those low sheds inside blackening oak
the cider god waits to send mad its worshippers
and floor its courtiers like pigs in straw.

On the moor blackberries turn to nipples of wine,
cathedrals of fruit overhang hawthorn and willow.
The rhynes shrink back to black ditches
and stink worse than angry cattle stung by hips and haws,
trampling yellow flags and reed mace.

Our boots on the drove roads kick up dust
and we plod along. Dumb. Thirsty as sunbaked clods,
starting up deer and the lone harrier,
v-shaped in the haze hangs under the sky:
ultimate summer.

Mushrooming at Stoke St. Gregory

Up on the arid ridge a mild gulf of air, warm and damp.
Just after sundown, a static afterglow,
where the moor is a huge lantern low on its wick.
The fields speak a long battered history
while I dodge thistles and cowpats,
breathing in the cidery silage stink of beast.

They are lying on the dung edges
big and broad, Saxon shield bosses,
patiently lifted out of growth with that sucking squelch
and gathered up as gently as old manuscript.
Clear water takes off the taints of pasture.
Under the knife, they render to impossible strips of flesh,
redolent of the earth's voice
oozing an unreadable black ink.

A Cider Brandy
For the Burrow Hill cider makers

In my warm glass I scent
the bones of this farmhouse.

Deep ages of fruit-laden avenues –
walking back under thick blossom.

(A copper still from Picardy
formed these narratives and images).

And for me, all Somerset catches
on my tongue and throat.

Something exhaled from the red earth,
the outbreathings and leachings of the golden
                              apple past.
Orchards of memory, giving birth at last.